All Kinds of

FRIENDS

Shelley Rotner & Sheila M. Kelly

M Millbrook Press/Minneapolis

To all children who are discovering ways
to make different friends —S.K.

To my dear friend Sheila —S.R.

Text copyright © 2018 by Shelley Rotner and Sheila M. Kelly
Photographs copyright © 2018 by Shelley Rotner

Millbrook Press
A division of Lerner Publishing Group, Inc.
241 First Avenue North
Minneapolis, MN 55401 USA

For reading levels and more information, look up this title at
www.lernerbooks.com.

Additional images: © iStockphoto.com/ulimi (pattern).

Designed by Kimberly Morales.
Main body text set in Futura Std Bold Condensed 28/39.
Typeface provided by Adobe Systems.

Library of Congress Cataloging-in-Publication Data

Names: Rotner, Shelley, author, illustrator. | Kelly, Sheila M., author.
Title: All kinds of friends / Shelley Rotner & Sheila Kelly.
Description: Minneapolis : Millbrook Press, [2017]
Identifiers: LCCN 2016053696 (print) | LCCN 2017007213 (ebook) |
    ISBN 9781512431056 (lb : alk. paper) | ISBN 9781512451115 (eb pdf)
Subjects: LCSH: Friendship—Juvenile literature.
Classification: LCC BF575.F66 R68 2017 (print) | LCC BF575.F66 (ebook)
    | DDC 177/.62—dc23

LC record available at https://lccn.loc.gov/2016053696

Manufactured in the United States of America
1-41663-23515-2/7/2017

There are all kinds of friends.

Young friends, old friends.

New friends, best friends,

family friends,

and more friends
next door.

Smart friends,

funny friends.

Furry friends and
feathered friends too.

**Small friends,
tall friends.**

Friends with different ways to walk.

Friends with different ways to talk.

Friends with different faces and families from different places.

School friends

and after-school friends.

Friends who play sports and all sorts of games.

Friends who like to dress up and friends who like to pretend.

Sometimes friends can make you sad

or even mad!

Mostly, friends have fun and like to be together.

Good friends, true friends
are the best friends of all.

What kinds of friends do you have?